Legal & Disclaimer

application of any of the information provided by this guide. This disclaimer applies to any damages or injury caused by the use and application, whether directly or indirectly, of any advice or information presented, whether for breach of contract, tort, negligence, personal injury, criminal intent, or under any other cause of action.

You agree to accept all the risks of using the information presented inside this book. You need to consult a professional medical practitioner in order to ensure you are both able & healthy enough to participate in this program.

Contents

Introduction

If you are trying to be wiser with your diet, beans are your best bet. They are cheap, delicious, and nutritious. They provide variety in your protein sources, they are rich in fiber, and they are low fat too. Beans are good substitute for meat.

Beans are easy to cook, but they are practical. You can make soups, chilies, and casseroles out of beans. Sometimes, when you have left-overs, you can use them as fillings in tacos, burritos, and enchiladas. As long as your kitchen contains plenty of seasonings, you will never run out of dishes you can make with beans.

Although beans are easy to cook, sometimes you have to boil them for hours. Canned beans are, of course, easy to prepare, but dry beans require long hours to soften. Navy beans and small beans cook the longest. The large white ones cook faster. The colored spotted beans contain the most distinct taste, but they cook longer than the white beans. As a rule of thumb, dry beans need to be soaked overnight or at least an hour to prepare them. With the use of Instant Pot, however, cooking time is reduced to around 30-45 minutes.

If you are looking for beans recipes, you have come to the right book. This book provides you with very easy to follow recipes using an Instant Pot.

Chapter 1: 20 Light, hearty meals to cook at home

1. Appalachian Soup Beans

Serves: 8

Cook Time: 20 minutes

Ingredients:

- 4 chopped strips of uncooked bacon
- 1 medium onion, diced
- 1 tablespoon garlic, minced
- ½ teaspoon cayenne pepper
- 1 ham hock
- 6 cups chicken broth
- 1 pound of dry-soaked pinto beans
- ¾ teaspoon kosher salt

Directions:

Soak the beans in a basin of water overnight for 8 or 9 hours. Pre-soaked beans cook faster. You can also soak quickly by using your Instant Pot. Put the beans in the Instant Pot with 4 cups of water. Press the "Sauté" button and bring to a boil. When the water is already boiling, close the lid by moving the valve to seal. Choose Manual/Pressure Cook option and set the timer to 2 minutes. Once the time is up, release the steam. Do not let the foam escape. If it escapes, seal the lid again for 20 seconds. Open the lid. Rinse and drain the beans.

Procedure

1) Turn on your Instant Pot and press the Sauté button fter pouring chopped bacon. Put the chopped bacon and sauté for a while. When the bacon is already crispy, remove it using a slotted spoon. Set aside.
2) Put the onions and stir for 5 minutes. Add the garlic and sauté for another 20 seconds.
3) Turn off the Instant Pot. Combine the bacon, cayenne pepper, ham hock, chicken broth and pinto beans with the sautéed onion and garlic.
4) Close the lid and turn the valve to Sealing. Click the Pressure Cook button and set it to 20 minutes.
5) Let the pot rest for 10 minutes and release the steam. Then open the lid.

6) Sprinkle salt and pepper to taste. Then shred the ham hock.

7) Serve the dish in bowls.

2. Bean and Bacon Soup

Serves: 6-8 people

Cook Time: 1 hour, 30 minutes

Bean soaking time: 8 hours

Ingredients:

- 1 pound of dry Great Northern white beans, soaked overnight
- 5 ounces of bacon, cut into 1/2-inch wide pieces
- 2 cups of onion, chopped
- 3/4 cup of celery, chopped
- 3/4 cup of carrots, chopped
- 3 cloves of garlic, minced

- 6 cups chicken stock
- 2 bay leaves
- 1 tablespoon fresh thyme
- 2 1/2 teaspoons kosher salt
- 1/4 teaspoon black pepper
- 3 tablespoon tomato paste
- 1/2 teaspoon paprika
- 1 ounce bacon, cooked and crumbled for garnish (optional)
- 2 tablespoon chopped fresh parsley for garnish (optional)

Directions:

Soak the beans in a basin of water overnight for 8-9 hours to cook faster. If you were not able to soak them overnight, you can boil them. Do a quick soak using your Instant Pot. Put the beans in the Instant Pot with 4 cups of water. Press the Sauté button and bring to a boil. When the water is already boiling, close the lid by moving the valve to seal. Choose Manual/Pressure Cook option and set the timer to 2 minutes. Once the time is up, release the steam. Do not let the foam escape. If it escapes, seal the lid again for 20 seconds. Open the lid. Rinse and drain the beans.

Procedure

1) Drain the beans: Drain the beans that have been soaking overnight. For boiled beans drain the water immediately after boiling

2) Cook the bacon and vegetables: Put the bacon into a large (5 to 6 quart) thick-bottomed Dutch oven on medium high heat. Let the bacon cook for a minute or two to start rendering out some of its fat, then add the chopped onion, celery, and carrots.

3) Lower the heat to low, cover and cook for 12 to 15 minutes, until vegetables are completely cooked through and softened. Add the garlic and cook a minute more.

4) Add beans, stock, seasonings and simmer: Add the drained beans to the pot. Add the stock, the bay leaves, thyme, salt and pepper.

5) Increase heat to high to bring to a simmer, then lower the heat to maintain a simmer, partially covered, for 1 hour or until the beans are very soft.

6) Add tomato paste and paprika: Stir in the tomato paste and the paprika. Cook for 5 more minutes.

7) Purée half the soup: Remove the bay leaves. Using an immersion blender, purée half of the soup. You don't want the soup to be perfectly

smooth, but you want to purée enough of it so that the beans create a creamy base.

8) Add more salt and pepper to taste.
9) Garnish with crumbled cooked bacon and chopped parsley to serve.

3. Chicken and White Bean Soup

Serves: 8

Cook Time: 40 minutes

Ingredients:

- 1 tablespoon olive oil
- 1 yellow onion, diced
- 4 garlic cloves, minced
- 6 cups chicken broth
- 3 large carrots, peeled and cut into 1/2 inch pieces

- 3 ribs of celery, cut into 1/2 inch pieces
- 1 pound dry navy beans, rinsed and sorted
- 1 bay leaf
- 1 teaspoon dried rosemary
- 1/2 teaspoon dried thyme
- 1/2 teaspoon smoked paprika
- 1/4 teaspoon black pepper
- 1 1/4 teaspoon salt
- 2 boneless skinless chicken breasts uncooked (frozen is fine)
- 1 cup half and half (half cream, half whole milk)

Directions:

1) Turn on your Instant Pot and press the Sauté button. Drizzle the oil. Sauté the onion for 3 minutes. Add in the garlic and sauté for another 30 seconds. Pour the chicken broth and stir.
2) Put the carrots, celery, navy beans, bay leaf, rosemary, thyme, smoked paprika, pepper and salt. Stir.
3) Close the lid and rotate the valve to Sealing. Click the Manual/Pressure Cook button. Cook on high pressure. Set it to 33 minutes.
4) Let the pot rest for 5 minutes and release the steam. Then open the lid.

5) Transfer the chicken to a cutting board to shred.

6) Once done, put the shredded chicken back to the pot.

7) Warm the cup of half and half in a microwave for a minute. Pour it to the chicken and Stir.

8) Add salt and peppcr to taste.

9) Serve in bowls.

4. Chili with White Beans, Pork, and Green Chiles

Serves: 6

Cook Time: 1 hour, 20 minutes

Ingredients:

- 1 tablespoon olive oil
- 1 1/2 pounds ground pork
- 2 (4.5-oz.) cans chopped green chillies, drained
- 1 medium-size white onion, chopped
- 1 large poblano chili, seeded and chopped
- 2 teaspoons chopped garlic
- 2 teaspoons ground cumin
- 1 1/4 teaspoons kosher salt
- 1/2 teaspoon black pepper
- 1/2 pound dry cannellini beans
- 4 cups unsalted chicken stock
- 2 tablespoons lime juice
- 1 medium-size ripe avocado, sliced
- 2 ounces Monterey Jack cheese, shredded
- 2 tablespoons chopped fresh cilantro

Directions and procedure:

1) Turn on your Instant Pot and press the Sauté button and set high heat . Drizzle oil to the ground pork and sauté for 6 minutes and transfer to plate when ready.
2) Put green chilies, onion, poblano, garlic, cumin, salt, and pepper to the pot. Cook for 6 minutes. Stir occasionally until the vegetables are tender.

3) Pour the stock to the pot and add in the beans and pork.
4) Close the lid and move the valve to Sealing. Press the Manual/Pressure Cook button and set it to High Pressure. Cook it for 50 minutes.
5) When the time is up, release the steam.
6) Remove the lid. Drizzle some lime juice and Stir.
7) Serve in bowls. Garnish with avocado, cheese, and cilantro.

5. Colombian-Style Red Beans

Serves: 8

Cook Time: 1 hour

Ingredients:

- 1 tablespoon canola oil
- 2 ounces fresh Mexican chorizo, casings removed
- 1 medium-size yellow onion, chopped
- 1 medium-size red bell pepper, chopped
- 3 garlic cloves, chopped
- 3 plum tomatoes, chopped
- 2 teaspoons achiote paste
- 2 teaspoons ground cumin
- 1 1/4 teaspoons kosher salt
- 2 1/2 cups unsalted chicken stock
- 1/2 pounds dried red kidney beans
- 2 tablespoons chopped fresh cilantro

Directions and procedure:

1) Turn on your Instant Pot and press the Sauté button. Set it to Normal heat. Drizzle oil and Sauté the chorizo for 4 minutes. Once the chorizo is brown, add in onion, bell pepper, and garlic.
2) As soon as the vegetables are already tender, add in the tomatoes, achiote paste, cumin, and salt. Cook for another 5 minutes and stir occasionally.
3) Pour the chicken stock and add in the beans.

4) Close the lid and move the valve to Seal. Press the Manual/Pressure Cook button and set it to High Pressure. Cook it for 45 minutes.
5) Use the quick-release option to release the steam from the cooker. Carefully open the lid.
6) Serve in bowls. Garnish with cilantro, parsley, or basil leaves.

6. Creamy Rich Mexican Refried Beans

Serves: 6

Cook Time: 55 minutes

Ingredients:

- 2 cups dry pinto beans
- 7 cups water
- 1/2 yellow onion, cut into 1-inch chunks
- 3 garlic cloves
- 1 teaspoon dried oregano
- 1 tablespoon lime juice
- 1 1/2 teaspoon salt
- 1 teaspoon cumin
- 1/4 cup cotija cheese, crumbled

Directions:

1) Rinse the dry beans in a strainer and pour them in the Instant Pot.
2) Pour water in pot and add the onions, garlic, oregano, cumin, and salt.
3) Close the lid and rotate the valve to Seal. Press the Beans button and set it to 35 minutes.
4) Once the time is up, use the natural release option to release the steam from the cooker. This may take 15 minutes.
5) Let the beans cool and transfer to a blender. Do not throw the beans water away.
6) Drizzle some lime juice on the beans and season with salt. As you blend the beans gradually add beans water to the mixture to get desired thickness.

7) The dish is done when it is already smooth. Sprinkle cotija cheese on top.
8) Serve with Mexican Rice or enchiladas.

Storage: Let the refried beans completely cool. Place it in an airtight container. Store it in the fridge up to 3 days. You may also freeze the beans in an airtight bag. It can last for 60 days. If you are ready to cook it, reheat the beans in a pan.

7. Instant Pot New Orleans-Style Red Beans and Rice

Serves: 6-8

Cook Time: 1 hour

Ingredients:

- 1 tablespoon oil
- 1 pound smoked sausage, sliced
- 1/4 stick of butter
- 2 cups chopped onions, celery, green bell peppers, and parsley flakes
- 1 clove garlic, chopped
- 1 package Camellia Brand Red Kidney Beans
- 6 cups water
- 1 bay leaf
- salt
- pepper
- cajun seasoning

Directions:

1) Rinse the beans in a basin.
2) Turn on your Instant Pot and press the Sauté button. Drizzle oil and Sauté the sliced sausage for 5 minutes. When the sausage is already brown, transfer it to a plate lined with a paper towel.
3) Put a stick of butter to the Instant Pot and add   chopped onions, celery, green bell peppers, parsley flakes, and garlic. Cook until the vegetables are soft.

4) Add the cooked sausage to the pot. Pour water and toss in the beans and bay leaf and Stir occasionally.

5) Turn off the Sauté setting. Close the lid and rotate the valve to Sealing. Set the Manual/Pressure Cook button on High Pressure and Cook it for 40 minutes.

6) When the time is up, use the Natural Release option. It should take 20 minutes to release the steam. Slowly open the lid.

7) Mash the beans until you achieve the desired consistency. Sprinkle salt, pepper, and Cajun seasoning to taste.

8) Serve with hot cooked rice.

8. White Bean Chili

Serves: 8-10

Cook Time: 1 hour

Ingredients:

- 1 tablespoon oil
- 1 onion, chopped
- 3 cloves garlic, minced
- 1 can of green chilies, chopped
- 1 teaspoon cumin
- 1 teaspoon smoked paprika
- 1 teaspoon chipotle chili powder
- ½ teaspoon kosher salt
- 1-pound Camellia Brand Great Northern Beans
- 6 cups chicken broth
- 1 pound boneless, skinless chicken thighs
- 1 ½ cups frozen corn kernels
- Salt and pepper to taste
- chopped fresh cilantro, green onions, avocado and shredded cheddar cheese (optional)

Directions and preparation: Soak the beans in a basin of water overnight or do a quick soak by putting beans and four cups of water and sauté in instant pot. Pre-soaked beans cook faster. Press the Sauté button and bring to a boil. When the water is already boiling, close the lid by moving the valve to seal. . Choose Manual/Pressure Cook option and set the timer to 2 minutes. Once the time is up, release the steam. Do not let the foam escape. If it escapes, seal the lid again for 20 seconds. Open the lid. Rinse and drain the beans.

Procedure:

1) Rinse and drain the beans in a strainer.
2) Turn on your Instant Pot and press the Sauté button. Drizzle oil. Sauté the chopped onion until it is translucent. Add in the garlic, green chilies, cumin, smoked paprika, and chipotle chili powder.
3) Pour the broth and add in the beans and chicken and Stir.
4) Turn off the Sauté function. Close the lid and rotate the valve to Sealing. Press Manual/Pressure Cook option. Set to High Pressure for 40 minutes.
5) As soon as the time is up, use the natural release option. It should take 20 minutes to release the steam from the cooker. Rotate the valve to Venting.
6) Slowly open the lid. Stir. Transfer the big chunks of chicken in a cutting board and shred the chicken. Put the shredded chicken back into the pot.
7) Add in the frozen corn and stir. Season salt and pepper to taste.
8) Serve the soup in a bowl. Top it with chopped fresh cilantro, green onions, avocado and shredded cheddar cheese.

9. Instant Pot Charro Beans

Serves: 6-8

Cook Time: 1 hour

Ingredients:

- 1 pound dried pinto beans, rinsed
- 8 ounces of bacon, chopped
- ¼ cup yellow onion, diced
- 1 jalapeno, seeds removed, diced
- 2 teaspoons sea salt
- 1 teaspoon cumin
- 2 teaspoons roasted minced garlic
- 1 can fire roasted or diced
- 5 cups chicken stock or broth
- 2 bay leaves

Directions:

1) Turn on your Instant Pot and press the Sauté button. Set it to high heat. Drizzle oil. Sauté the bacon until it is crispy. Toss in the onion, garlic, and jalapeno. Stir for another 1-2 minutes.

2) Pour the chicken broth. Stir in salt, tomatoes, beans, cumin and bay leaves.

3) Close the lid and press Manual/Pressure Cook option on High. Set the timer to 60 minutes.

4) Use the Natural Release option to release the steam from the cooker for about 30-40 minutes.

5) Stir well and Serve in bowls.

10. Instant Pot Rice and Beans

Serves: 5

Cook Time: 25 minutes

Ingredients:

- 1 1/4 cup dry red kidney beans
- 1 1/2 cup dry brown rice
- 1 cup salsa
- ½ cup cilantro, chopped
- 3 cups vegetable broth
- 2 cups water

Directions:

1) Separate leaves and stems of cilantro and chop the leaves.
2) Put the dried beans and rice to the Instant Pot.
3) Pour vegetable broth and waterand Stir to Mix all the ingredients well.
4) Toss in the salsa and cilantro stems into the pot. Leave them on top of the rice and beans and do not mix them.
5) Close the lid and rotate the valve to Sealing. Press the Manual/Pressure Cook button and set it to 25 minutes. Cook on High pressure.
6) Use the Natural Release option. It should take another 10 minutes to release the steam. Rotate the valve to Venting.
7) Serve the beans and rice in bowls. Sprinkle some chopped cilantro leaves on top.

11. Instant Pot Sausage and White Beans

Serves: 6-8

Cook Time: 1 hour and 10 minutes

Ingredients:

- 2 teaspoon olive oil
- 1 1/2 pounds smoked kielbasa sausage, sliced in 1-inch thick rounds
- 1 large yellow onion, chopped
- 1 large bay leaf
- 4 carrots, chopped
- 3 celery stalks, chopped
- 4 sprigs fresh thyme
- 4-inch long sprig of fresh rosemary
- 1/4 teaspoon oregano, dried
- 4 cloves garlic, pressed or minced
- 1/2 teaspoon pepper

- 6 cups chicken broth, low sodium
- 1 pound dry navy beans
- 3 cups fresh baby spinach or chopped kale (optional)
- salt to taste

Directions:

1) Turn on your Instant Pot and press the Sauté button. Set it to high heat. Drizzle oil. Sauté the sausage until it is brown on all sides.
2) Add onion, bay leaf, carrots and celery. Cook until the vegetables are tender. Then deglaze the bottom of the pot.
3) Toss in the thyme, rosemary, oregano, and garlic. Cook for another minute.
4) Pour the broth and sprinkle pepper. Stir well.
5) Cover the pot and let the broth simmer.
6) Put the beans and stir well. Close the lid and move the valve to Sealing. Press the Manual/Pressure Cook button and set it to High Pressure. Cook it for 40 minutes.
7) When the time is up, use the Natural Release option. It should take 15 minutes to release the pressure from the cooker. Let the pot cool. Rotate the valve to Venting.
8) Slowly open the lid. Check if the beans are already tender. In case the beans are not yet soft, cook them for another 5 minutes. Keep

the high pressure. Use Natural Release for another 10-15 minutes.

9) When the beans are ready, stir gently and Season with salt to taste. Add the optional ingredients, spinach or kale and Stir them.

10) Serve it in bowls with bread on the side.

12. Madras Lentils with Ground Beef

Serves: 6

Cook Time: 10 minutes

Ingredients:

- 1 pound lean ground beef or ground turkey
- 1 cup diced yellow onion
- 1 jalapeno, minced (seeds and pith removed)
- 1 tablespoon garlic
- 2 cups chicken or beef broth

- 2 teaspoon smoked paprika
- 2 teaspoon cumin
- ½ teaspoon ground coriander
- ⅛ teaspoon ground ginger
- 1 teaspoon sugar
- 1 teaspoon salt
- ½ teaspoon pepper
- 14.5 oz. can red kidney beans, rinsed and drained
- 1 cup uncooked brown lentils
- 8 oz. can tomato sauce
- 3 tablespoon tomato paste
- 1 tablespoon red wine vinegar
- ½ cup half and half
- grated cheese and diced green onions (toppings)

Directions:

1) Turn on your Instant Pot and press the Sauté button and set it to high heat. Drizzle oil and Sauté the ground beef or turkey for 5 minutes until it turns is brown. Toss in the onion and jalapeno. Stir for several minutes and add the garlic. Sauté for another 30 seconds.
2) Pour the broth and put in paprika, cumin, coriander, ginger, sugar, salt, pepper, beans and lentils. Stir the mixture well.

3) Next, put the tomato sauce and paste and do not blend.
4) Close the lid and move the valve to Sealing. Press the Manual/Pressure Cook button and set it to High Pressure. Cook it for 10 minutes.
5) Use the Quick-Release option. Rotate the valve to Venting to release the remaining steam from the cooker. Slowly open the lid.
6) Drizzle the vinegar and the cup of half and half. Season salt and pepper to taste.
7) Serve in bowls topped with grated cheddar and diced green onions. You may also use it as rice toppings.

13. Mung Bean Stew

Serves: 5-8

Cook Time: 30-40 minutes

Ingredients:

- 3/4 cup dry whole green mung beans
- ½ brown basmati rice
- ½ teaspoon coconut oil
- ½ teaspoon cumin seeds
- ½ red onion, chopped
- 28 oz. crushed tomatoes
- 5 cloves of garlic
- 1 inch ginger, peeled
- 1 teaspoon turmeric
- 1 teaspoon ground coriander
- ½ teaspoon garam masala

- ½ teaspoon cayenne
- ¼ teaspoon black pepper
- 4 cups water
- 1 teaspoon lemon juice
- ¾ teaspoon salt

Directions:

Soak the beans in a basin of water at least 15 minutes before you cook. Overnight soaking is better. Soak the brown rice in a separate bowl for 15 minutes. Pre-soaked beans and rice cook faster.

Procedure

1) Put onions, tomatoes, garlic, ginger, spices and 2 tablespoons of water in a blender. Pulse a few times until all ingredients are pureed.
2) Turn on your Instant Pot and press the Sauté button. Drizzle oil. Toast the cumin seeds for 1 minute. Pour the puree of spices onto the Instant Pot. Cook the mixture for 15 minutes. Turn off the pot when the cooking time is up.
3) Meanwhile, drain the beans and rice. Put them into the Instant Pot. Add the cups of water and lemon juice. Sprinkle some saltand Stir well.
4) Close the lidby rotating the valve to Seal . Press Manual/Pressure Cook option and set the timer to 15 minutes.

5) When the cooking cycle is up, use the Natural Release option. It should take a few minutes to release the steam from the cooker.
6) Serve in bowls with a bread or cracker. You may also top sliced jalapeño and chopped cilantro leaves.

14. Pinto Beans with Chorizo

Serves: 6

Cook Time: 1 hour, 15 minutes

Ingredients:

- 1 tablespoon cooking oil
- 4 oz. dry (Spanish) chorizo
- 1 yellow onion, diced
- 3 cloves garlic, minced
- 2 cups dry pinto beans
- 2 bay leaves
- Freshly cracked pepper
- 3 cups reduced sodium chicken broth
- 15 oz. can dice tomatoes

Directions:

1) Slice the chorizo into small dice. Turn on the Instant Pot and press the Sauté buttonand set it to Normal heat. Drizzle oil and Sauté the chorizo until it becomes crispy on the edges. Add the onion and garlic. Sauté until the onions are translucent.
2) Put the beans, bay leaves, and pepper to the pot. Cook the beans for several minutes.
3) Pour the broth and stir the mixture. Close the lid and move the valve to Sealing. Press the Manual/Pressure Cook button and set it to High Pressure. Cook it for 35 minutes.
4) When the cooking cycle is complete, use the Natural Release option to release the steam. It should take several minutes until the steam is fully released.

5) Slowly open the lid to remove the bay leaf. Pour the can of diced tomatoes and stir well.

6) Close the lid and move the valve to Sealing. Press the Sauté button and set it to Normal. Let it simmer. Stir often. Cook until the beans are tender and sauce is thickened.

7) Serve the beans with bowl of rice, side it with tortillas and chips. You may also top it with cheese, cilantro, and onions.

15. Red Beans

Serves: 6

Cook Time: 1 hour, 25 minutes

Ingredients:

- 1/2 pound smoked sausage, sliced in small pieces
- 1 tablespoon olive oil
- 1 onion, finely diced
- 1 bell pepper, finely diced
- 3 stalks celery, finely diced
- 4 cloves garlic, minced
- 1 pound dry red beans, uncooked
- 1 teaspoon dried thyme
- 1 teaspoon dried oregano
- 1 teaspoon smoked paprika
- 1/4 teaspoon cayenne
- Fresh ground black pepper
- 3 cups chicken broth
- 2 cups water
- 3 green onions, sliced
- 6 cups cooked rice

Directions:

1) Turn on your Instant Pot and press the Sauté buttonand Set it to high heat. Drizzle oil, Sauté the smoked sausage for 6 minutes. When the sausage is already brown, transfer it to a plate.
2) Put the onion, bell pepper, celery, and garlic to the pot. Sauté for 5 minutes or until the onion is translucent.
3) Wash the beans and remove small debris and dirt. When the beans are already clean, mix them with the sausage. Then season the mixture with thyme, thyme, oregano, paprika, cayenne, and fresh ground black pepper. Add in the chicken broth and water,stir well to combine all ingredients.
4) Close the lid and move the valve to Sealing. Press the Manual/Pressure Cook button and set it to High Pressure. Cook it for 35 minutes.
5) Use the Natural Release option to release the steam from the cooker.
6) Check the beans if they are already soft enough to eat. You may cook them for another 20 minutes if they are not yet soft.
7) When the beans are already soft, smash them using the back of a spoon. The consistency should be thick. Season it with salt.

8) Serve this red bean dish with a bowl of rice. Top it with green onions.

16. Smoky Lentils and Rice

Serves: 10

Cook Time: 40 minutes

Ingredients:

- 4 cups vegetable broth
- 2 cups long grain brown rice
- 2 cups French green lentils
- 2 tablespoons smoked paprika
- 2 teaspoons fennel seeds
- 2 teaspoons onion powder
- 1 teaspoon granulated garlic powder
- 1 teaspoon black pepper

- 1 teaspoon kosher salt
- 1 tablespoon apple cider vinegar

Directions:

1) Combine all the ingredients in the Instant Pot except the vinegar. Stir well.
2) Close the lid and move the valve to Sealing. Press the Manual/Pressure Cook button and set it to High Pressure. Cook it for 16 minutes.
3) When the cooking cycle is over, release steam by pressing "natural release button" for around 16 minutes. Rotate the valve on the lid to Venting to release the pressure from the cooker.
4) Slowly open the lid. Add the apple cider vinegar and Stir well. Season with salt to taste.
5) Serve the dish in a bowl.

Storage: You may store the leftover in a refrigerator, and it should last for days. The dish becomes dry though. Reheat the leftover when you serve it again. If the dish is too dry, add olive oil before you reheat the lentils.

17. Spicy Brown Rice Black Bean Salad

Serves: 4-8

Cook Time: 40 minutes

Ingredients:

- 1 cup brown rice
- 1 1/2 cups water
- 1/4 teaspoon salt
- 14 oz. can black beans, drained and rinsed
- 12 grape tomatoes, quartered
- 1 avocado, diced
- 1/4 cup cilantro, minced
- 3 tablespoons fresh lime juice

- 2 teaspoons Cholula or Tabasco
- 2 garlic cloves, minced or pressed
- 1 teaspoon agave nectar
- 1/8 teaspoon salt
- 3 tablespoons extra virgin olive oil

Directions:

1) Put the rice in the Instant Pot, pour water, and add some salt. Close the lid and move the valve to Sealing. Press the Manual/Pressure Cook button and set it to High Pressure to cook it for 24 minutes.
2) When the cooking cycle is finished, use the Natural Release option to release the steam from the cooker. Wait for 10 minutes, and then press the Quick Release button. As soon as the valve drops, slowly open the lid. Check if the rice is cooked. Allow the rice to cool.
3) Dressing: In a bowl, mix the lime juice, tabasco, garlic, agave, and salt. Whisk while pouring olive oil gradually.
4) As soon as the rice cools down, in a large bowl, combine it with black beans, tomato, avocado, and cilantro. Add the dressing. Stir well to mix combine all the ingredients.
5) Serve the dish in bowls.

18. Tacos with Smoky Lentils

Serves: 16

Cook Time: 25 minutes

Ingredients:

- 2 cups dry lentils, green or brown
- 4 cups low-sodium chicken/vegetable broth
- 1/2 cup salsa
- 1 teaspoon onion powder
- 1 teaspoon garlic powder
- 1 teaspoon chili powder
- 1/2 teaspoon cumin
- Corn or flour tortillas, for serving
- shredded cheese
- 14.5 ounce can diced tomatoes
- avocado, chopped (or guacamole)

- Fresh cilantro
- Green onion , chopped
- Olives
- Plain Greek yogurt/sour cream
- salsa or hot sauce

Directions:

1) Combine all the ingredients in the Instant Pot. Stir well.
2) Close the lid and move the valve to Sealing. Press the Manual/Pressure Cook button and set it to High Pressure. Cook it for 15 minutes.
3) When the cooking cycle is over, use the Quick-Release option to release the steam from the cooker. Slowly open the lid.
4) Serve the dish in bowls. Top it with tortillas, shredded cheese, tomatoes, chopped avocado, cilantro, green onion, olives, sour cream, and salsa.

19. Tex-Mex Chicken and Black Bean Soup

Serves: 5

Cook Time: 25 minutes

Ingredients:

- 1 1/4 pounds boneless, skinless chicken thighs
- 4 cups unsalted chicken stock
- 15-oz. can unsalted black beans, drained and rinsed
- 14.5-oz. can unsalted diced tomatoes
- 1 cup chopped yellow onion
- 1 cup chopped red or orange bell pepper
- 1 cup fresh or frozen corn kernels

- 2 tablespoons chipotle chilies in adobo sauce, chopped
- 2 garlic cloves, minced
- 2 teaspoons chili powder
- 2 teaspoons ground cumin
- 3/4 teaspoon kosher salt
- 1/4 teaspoon black pepper
- 2 tablespoons fresh lime juice
- 1/2 cup plain whole-milk Greek yogurt
- 1/2 cup fresh cilantro leaves

Directions:

1) In an Instant Pot, combine the following: chicken thighs, chicken stock, beans, tomatoes, onion, bell pepper, corn, chilies, garlic, chili powder, cumin, salt, and black pepper. Stir well.
2) Close the lid and move the valve to Sealing. Press the Manual/Pressure Cook button and set it to High Pressure. Cook it for 10 minutes.
3) When the cooking cycle is over, rotate the valve to Venting. Use the Quick Release option to release the steam from the cooker.
4) Slowly open the lid. Place the chicken to a cutting board and shred it. Put the shredded chicken back to the Instant Pot

and add some drops of lime juicewhile stirring.

5) Serve in bowls. Add yogurt and cilantro as toppings.

20. Tuscan White Bean and Lentil Soup

Serves: 6

Cook Time: 25 minutes

Ingredients:

- 4 cups low-sodium vegetable broth
- 2 (15-oz.) cans unsalted Great Northern beans, drained and rinsed
- 1 cup uncooked brown or green lentils, rinsed
- 1-2 cups water
- 1 cup chopped yellow onion
- 3/4 cup chopped carrot
- 1 Parmesan cheese rind
- 2 garlic cloves, minced
- 1 teaspoon fresh thyme leaves
- 1/2 teaspoon black pepper
- 1/4 teaspoon kosher salt
- 1 bay leaf
- 4 cups rainbow chard, coarsely chopped
- 2 tablespoons fresh lemon juice
- 2 ounces Parmesan cheese, grated

Directions:

1) In an Instant Pot, combine the following: vegetable broth, beans, lentils, 2 cups water, onion, carrot, Parmesan rind, garlic, thyme, pepper, salt, and bay leaf. Stir well.
2) Close the lid and move the valve to Sealing. Press the Manual/Pressure Cook button and set it to High Pressure. Cook it for 15 minutes.
3) When the cooking cycle is over, rotate the valve to Venting. Use the Quick Release option to release the steam from the cooker.
4) Slowly open the lidand drizzle some lemon juice and add the chard. Stir well for about 2 minutes.
5) Remove the bay leaf and cheese rind.
6) Serve in bowls. Sprinkle Parmesan on top of the dish.

21. Black Bean Burrito Bowl

Serves: 6

Cook Time: 22 minutes

Ingredients:

- 2 cups long grain white rice
- 2-3 tablespoon olive oil
- 10 oz. can of diced tomatoes with green chilies
- 1 medium onion
- 4 cloves garlic
- 2 cups vegetable broth
- 1 teaspoon sea salt
- 2 (14 oz.) cans of black beans, drained and rinsed

Toppings:

- Avocado slices/guacamole!!
- Olives
- Diced tomato
- shredded lettuce
- shredded purple cabbage
- Freshly squeezed lemon
- Canned jalapeno slices
- Vegan sour cream

Directions:

1) Wash the rice in running water. Drain and set aside.
2) Turn on your Instant Pot and press the Sauté button. Set it to high heat. Drizzle olive oil and put the rice in the pot and cook for 5 minutes, occasionally stirring the rice. Scrape the bottom of the pan to remove the rice that sticks.
3) In the meantime, pour the can of diced tomatoes and chilies in an immersion blender. Add the garlic and onion. Then pour the vegetable brothand Stir well. Blend until the mixture is smooth.
4) Pour the mixture to the Instant Pot. Stir well. Cook for another 5 minutes.
5) After 5 minutes, add the black beans to the pot.

6) Close the lid and move the valve to Sealing. Press the Manual/Pressure Cook button and set it to Low Pressure. Cook it for 12 minutes.
7) Use the Natural Release option to release the steam from the cooker. It should take another 10 minutes to release the pressure.
8) Serve it in bowls. Put your favorite toppings.

22. Vegan Three Bean Chill

Serves: 8

Cook Time: 30 minutes

Ingredients:

- 2 tablespoon extra-virgin olive oil
- 1 small onion, finely chopped

- 2 large carrots, diced
- 2 stalks celery, chopped
- 3 cloves garlic, minced
- 1 15 oz. can black beans, rinsed and drained
- 1 15 oz. can cannellini beans, rinsed and drained
- 1 15 oz. can red kidney beans, rinsed and drained
- 1 cup corn, canned or fresh
- 2 cups vegetable broth
- 1 14.5 oz. can diced tomatoes
- 3 oz. tomato paste
- 3 tablespoon chili powder
- 1/2 teaspoon ground cumin
- 1/2 teaspoon kosher salt
- 1/4 teaspoon black pepper

Directions:

1) Turn on your Instant Pot and press the Sauté button. Set it to high heatand drizzle olive oil. Pour onions, celery, garlic, and carrotsand cook them for 3-5 minutes or until the vegetables are tender.

2) Add the beans, tomatoes, vegetable broth, tomato paste, chili powder, cumin, salt, and pepper.

3) Press the Cancel button. Close the lid and move the valve to Sealing. Press the Manual/Pressure Cook button and set it to High Pressure. Cook it for 2 minutes.
4) When the cooking cycle is finished, use the Natural Release option to release the pressure from the cooker. Rotate the valve to Venting. Let the cooker cool down.
5) Serve the dish in bowls. Top it with your favorite chili.

Storage: You may refrigerate the dish in an airtight container for 5 days, and freeze it up to 3 months. When you are ready to eat the dish, just reheat it.

23. Garlicky White Beans with Tomatoes

Serves: 6-8

Cook Time: 50 minutes

Ingredients:

- 3 tablespoons extra virgin olive oil
- 1 small yellow onion, diced
- 5 garlic cloves, minced
- 1 pound cannellini beans, rinsed
- 3 1/2 cups low sodium vegetable broth
- 28 ounce can crushed tomatoes
- 4 ounces tomato paste
- 1 1/2 teaspoons kosher salt, plus more to season
- 1 teaspoon crushed red pepper flakes
- Crumbled feta (for topping)

- Chopped basil (for topping)
- Crusty toast (for topping)

Directions:

1) Turn on your Instant Pot and press the Sauté button. Set it to high heat. Drizzle olive oil. Sauté the onion for 5 minutes or until the onion is translucent. Stir in the garlic and cook for another minute.
2) Turn off the Sauté function. Add the beans, broth, tomatoes, tomato paste, salt, and red pepper flakes. Refrain from stirring. The tomatoes should remain on top of the mixture, so it does not scorch at the bottom.
3) Close the lid and turn the valve to Sealing. Click the Manual/Pressure Cook button and set it to 40 minutes.
4) When the cooking cycle is done, use the Natural Release option to release the steam from the cooker. In case the beans are not yet cooked, cook for another 5 minutes. Repeat until the beans are cooked and tender.
5) Slowly open the lid. Stir the mixture, and add seasonings.
6) Serve the dish over bread. Add crumbled feta cheese and basil on top.

24. Instant Pot Green Beans

Serves: 2

Cook Time: 13 minutes

Ingredients:

- ½ pound green beans
- ½ cup cold water
- 1 tablespoon peanut oil or olive oil
- 4 garlic cloves, minced
- salt (optional)
- Fish sauce (optional)

Directions:

1) Pour a half cup of cold water in your Instant Pot. Put a steamer rack on top of the pot. Steam the green beans. Press the Manual/Pressure Cook button and set it to High Pressure. Cook it for 2 minutes. Use the Quick-Release option to release the steam from the cooker.
2) Transfer the green beans to a plate and let it cool.
3) Throw the water in the pot. Dry it using a towel.
4) When the pot is ready, turn on the Instant Pot and press the Sauté button. Drizzle some oil and toss in the minced garlic. Sauté for about 30 seconds. Add in the steamed green beans. Stir for another 30 seconds.
5) Season with salt and fish sauce. Stir consistently so all beans are coated evenly. Do not overcook the beans. It should still be a little crunchy when served.
6) Serve the stir fry beans while hot.

25. Instant Pot Green Beans and Potatoes

Serves: 6

Cook Time: 25 minutes

Ingredients:

- 8 slices bacon, chopped
- 1/2 red onion, chopped
- 1 clove garlic, minced
- 6-8 potatoes small Yukon Gold, halved
- 1 tablespoon butter
- 2 pounds Haricot Verts Fresh, trimmed (or Green Beans)
- 3/4 cup chicken broth
- Olive oil
- Salt and pepper, to taste
- Fresh parsley, chopped

Directions:

1) Turn on your Instant Pot and press the Sauté button. Drizzle some oil. Put the slices of bacon and sauté for a while. When the bacon is already crispy, remove it using a slotted spoon. Wrap it in a clean paper towel to remove the grease and set aside.
2) Sauté the garlic and onion until the onion is translucent.
3) Put the potatoes and cook until they are golden. Add more oil if needed.
4) When the potatoes are golden, stir in the butter.
5) Toss in the green beans. Stir well to make sure the beans and potatoes are coated evenly.
6) Pour the chicken broth. Close the lid and turn the valve to Sealing. Click the Manual/Pressure Cook button and set it to 6 minutes.
7) Use the Natural Release option to release the steam from the cooker.
8) Slowly open the lid. Season to taste. Then add the bacon. Stir well.
9) Serve in bowls. Top with chopped parsley for more freshness.

Storage: This dish can be stored in a refrigerator for 3-4 days.

Chapter 2: 10 Versatile Appetizers and Side Dishes

1. Black Bean Dip

Serves: 24

Cook Time: 45 minutes

Ingredients:

- 1.5 cups dried black beans
- 1 medium onion, diced
- 4 cloves garlic, minced
- 2 medium jalapeños, chopped
- 14.5 oz. canned crush tomatoes
- 1 and 3/4 cup vegetable broth
- 1.5 tablespoon avocado oil
- 1 tablespoon lime juice
- 2 teaspoon ground cumin
- 1 teaspoon smoked paprika
- 3/4 teaspoon sea salt
- 1/2 teaspoon chili powder
- 1/2 teaspoon ground coriander

Toppings: chopped tomatoes, sliced jalapeños, diced bell pepper, chopped red onion, cilantro, sour cream, Greek yogurt, salsa, Pico de gallo, guacamole

Directions:

1) Sort and wash the black beans. Drain them using a coriander. Put them in the Instant Pot.
2) Add in the chopped vegetables, minced garlic, tomatoes, broth, oil, lime juice, and spices.
3) Turn on your Instant Pot and press the Bean button. Close the lid and move the valve to Sealing. Press the Manual/Pressure Cook

button and set it to High Pressure. Cook it for 30 minutes.

4) Use the Natural Release option to release the steam. Then use the Quick-Release option to release the remaining pressure from the cooker.

5) Place the cooked beans in a food processor to blend until the mixture is creamy. Season to taste.

6) Serve in bowls.

2. Buttery Instant Pot Green Beans and Potatoes

Serves: 4

Cook Time: 14 minutes

Ingredients:

- 1 pound green beans, trimmed
- 1 pound red potatoes cut into fourths
- 1 yellow onion, chopped
- 2 garlic cloves, minced
- 3 tablespoon unsalted butter
- 1 cup chicken broth
- 2 teaspoon lemon pepper seasoning
- 1 teaspoon Italian seasoning
- 1 tablespoon fresh lemon juice
- Salt and pepper to taste

Directions:

1) Put all the ingredients in the Instant Pot Press the Manual/Pressure Cook button and set it to High Pressure and cook it for 10 minutes.
2) Use the Natural Release option to release the steam. Then use the Quick-Release option to release the remaining pressure from the cooker.
3) Top the dish with bacon and serve in bowls.

3. Homemade Instant Pot Chili

Serves: 8

Cook time: 1 hour

Ingredients:

- 2 cups dry pinto beans
- 1–2 tablespoons olive oil
- 1 onion, diced
- 1 pound ground organic beef, chicken, turkey or vegan TVP
- 4 cloves garlic
- 1 ½ teaspoons kosher salt
- ½ teaspoon pepper
- 1 tablespoons chili powder
- 1 tablespoon cumin
- 2 teaspoons dried Mexican oregano
- 14-ounce can diced or crushed tomatoes with juices
- Tablespoons tomato paste

- ½ cups beef, chicken or veggie broth
- 1 cup dark beer
- 1–3 tablespoons fresh jalapeño, finely chopped (optional)
- 1 tablespoon Worcestershire sauce (optional)
- 1 –2 teaspoons dark cocoa powder, (optional)
- 1–2 teaspoons smoked paprika (optional)
- Frozen corn or diced red bell pepper (optional)
- Garnishes: grated cheese, sour cream, cilantro, avocado, scallions

Directions:

1) Put the beans in the Instant Pot with 4 cups of water. Close the lid. Move the valve to Sealing. Choose Manual/Pressure Cook option and set the timer to 10 minutes. Once the time is up, manually release the steam. Open the lid. Rinse and drain the beans. Set aside.
2) Press the Sauté function. Set it to high heat. Drizzle oil and saute the onion until it is translucent. Put the garlic, ground meat, and soy crumbles. Stir continuously and break the meat.
3) Season the mixture with salt, pepper, oregano, and the rest of the spices. Stir   thoroughly.

4) Add in the diced tomatoes, tomato paste, broth, beer, and Worcestershire. Add any optional ingredients you prefer and stir well.

5) Add in the beans. Close the lid and move the valve to Sealing. Press the Manual/Pressure Cook button and set it to High Pressure. Cook it for 22 minutes.

6) When the cooking cycle is done, use the Natural Release option to release the steam from the cooker.

7) You may sprinkle a little corn flour if you want a thicker consistency of the dish. Stir well.

8) Season to taste.

9) Serve in bowls, and add the toppings.

4. Instant Pot Southern Style Green Beans and Bacon

Serves: 4

Cook Time: 10 minutes

Ingredients:

- 1 pound fresh green beans, cut and snipped in half
- 3-4 slices thick-cut bacon
- 1 clove garlic, minced (or to taste)
- 1/4 cup onion, diced
- 3/4 cup chicken broth
- 1/2-3/4 tsp. kosher salt (to taste)
- 1/4 teaspoon black pepper

- red pepper flakes or dashes of hot sauce (optional)

Directions:

1) Turn on your Instant Pot and press the Sauté button. Set it to high heat. Drizzle little oil. Cook the bacon for about 3 minutes.
2) Add the garlic and onion. Sauté until the onion is translucent.
3) Pour the chicken broth and add the green beans. Season the mixture with salt and black pepper.
4) Close the lid and move the valve to Sealing. Press the Manual/Pressure Cook button and set it to High Pressure. Cook it for 5 minutes.
5) Once the cooking cycle is done, use the Quick-Release option to release the steam from the cooker.
6) Serve in bowls.

5. Instant Pot Baked Beans

Serves: 4-6

Cook Time: 1 hour and 30 minutes

Ingredients:

- 16 ounces dry navy or pinto beans
- 8 cups water
- 1 teaspoon salt
- 8 slices bacon
- 1 yellow onion, finely chopped
- 1/2 red or green bell pepper, finely chopped
- 2/3 cup barbecue sauce
- 1/2 cup ketchup
- 2 tablespoons spicy brown mustard
- ¼ cup cider vinegar
- 1 teaspoon liquid smoke

- ½ cup light brown sugar
- 1/2 cup water

Directions:

1) Put the beans in the pot add water and season with salt and close the lid and move the valve to Sealing. Press the Manual/Pressure Cook button and set it to High Pressure. Cook it for 25 minutes. When the cooking cycle is done, use the Natural Release option to release the steam from the cooker.

2) Open the pot. Dispense the beans to a strainer. Rinse in cold water and set aside.

3) Press the Sauté button. Set it to high heat. Drizzle some oil and Sauté the bacon for several minutes until it turns brown and crispy. Remove some of the grease.

4) Toss in the bell pepper and onion. Stir until the onion is translucent.

5) Turn off the pot. Combine barbecue sauce, ketchup, mustard, vinegar, and liquid smoke with the mixture.

6) Put brown sugar, water and beans. Stir well.

7) Close the lid and move the valve to Sealing. Press the Manual/Pressure Cook button and set it to High Pressure. Cook it for 15 minutes.

8) When the cooking cycle is complete, use the Natural Release option to release the steam from the cooker.
9) Open the pot to stir.
10)   1Serve in bowls.

6. Instant Pot Cuban Black Beans

Serves: 8

Cook Time: 1 hour and 15 minutes

Ingredients:

- 1 pound dried black beans
- 1 tablespoon olive oil
- 1 cup chopped yellow onion
- 1 cup chopped red bell pepper

- 1 medium jalapeno pepper, seeded and finely chopped
- 3 medium garlic cloves, finely chopped
- 1 1/4 teaspoons kosher salt
- 1 teaspoon ground cumin
- 1 teaspoon ground coriander
- 1 teaspoon dried oregano
- 2 bay leaves
- 3 cups unsalted chicken stock
- 1 1/2 cups cherry tomatoes, halved
- 1/2 cup chopped cilantro leaves

Directions:

1) Wash the black beans. Drain and set aside.
2) Turn on your Instant Pot and press the Sauté button. Set it to high heat. Drizzle olive oil and sauté the onion, garlic, cumin, coriander, and oregano. Season it with salt and pepper. Stir until the onion is translucent.
3) Add the beans and pour the chicken stock. Put the bay leaves. Stir well.
4) Close the lid and move the valve to Sealing. Press the Manual/Pressure Cook button and set it to High Pressure. Cook it for 37 minutes.
5) Once the cooking cycle is complete, use the Natural Release option to release the steam from the cooker.

6) Turn off the pot.
7) Serve the dish in bowls. Put tomatoes and chopped cilantro leaves as toppings.

7. Instant Pot Drunken Beans

Serves: 8

Cook Time: 30 minutes

Ingredients:

- 6 slices bacon
- 1 cup onion, finely diced
- 1 cup green pepper, finely diced
- 1 Jalapeño pepper, finely diced
- 3 cloves garlic, minced
- 1 lb. dried pinto beans

- 1 can (14.5 oz.) diced tomatoes
- 12 oz. Mexican beer
- 3 cups chicken or vegetable stock
- 1-2 teaspoon kosher salt
- 1 teaspoon cumin
- 1/4 teaspoon black pepper

Directions:

1) Wash and drain the beans.
2) Turn on your Instant Pot and press the Sauté button. Set it to high heat. Drizzle oil and sauté the bacon for one minute. Stir in the onion, jalapeño, and green pepper for 3 minutes and add in the garlic and stir for another 30 seconds.
3) Add the beans, tomatoes, beer, and stock. Season with salt, pepper, and cumin and stir well.
4) Close the lid and move the valve to Sealing. Press the Manual/Bean/Chili button and set it to High Pressure. Cook it for 20 minutes.
5) When the cooking cycle is complete, use the Natural Release option to release the steam from the cooker.
6) Season the dish with salt and pepper. Allow the dish to cool.
7) Serve the dish in bowls, top with chopped cilantro.

8. Instant Pot Pinto Beans

Serves: 6

Cook Time: 1 hour and 10 minutes

Ingredients:

- 1 lb. pinto beans
- 6 cups water
- 1 teaspoon fine sea salt
- 1 small to medium onion, peeled and halved
- 2 bay leaves (optional)
- Cilantro for garnish

Directions:

1) 1Wash, drain and pour the pinto beans in the pot. Pour the water and season with salt and toss in the bay leaves and onions.
2) 2Turn on the pot. Close the lid and turn the valve to Sealing. Click the Manual/Pressure Cook button and set it to 40 minutes.
3) 3When the cooking cycle is complete, use the Quick-Release option to release the steam from the cooker.
4) 4Slowly open the lid. Remove the bay leaves. Stir well.
5) 5Serve the soup in bowls.

9. Mexican Bean Dip

Serves: 6

Cook Time: 60 minutes

Ingredients:

- 1 cup dry pinto beans
- 4 cups water
- 4-5 chilies de arbol, stem removed
- 1 teaspoon salt (or more to taste)
- 1 1/2 teaspoon chili powder
- Queso fresco (optional)

Directions:

1) Wash the pinto beans. Drain and put them in the pot. Pour the water and season with chilies de arbol.
2) Close the lid and move the valve to Sealing. Press the Manual/Pressure Cook button and set it to High Pressure. Cook it for 45 minutes.
3) When the cooking cycle is complete, use the Natural Release option to release the steam from the cooker. After that, use the Quick-Release option to release the remaining pressure.
4) Transfer the cooked beans in a blender and season with salt and chili powder, blend to get the desired consistency is achieved.
5) Serve in bowls with tortilla chips on the side. Top with Queso fresco.

10. Saucy Pinto Beans

Serves: 8

Cook Time: 31 minutes

Ingredients:

- 2 cups dry pinto beans
- 2 tablespoon avocado oil
- 1 large yellow onion, diced
- 1 medium jalapeño, diced
- 2 teaspoon minced garlic
- 3 1/2 cups chicken stock
- 8 oz. can tomato sauce
- 2 tablespoon chili powder
- 1 tablespoon yellow mustard
- 1 teaspoon dried oregano
- 1 teaspoon cumin
- 1/2 teaspoon black pepper

- 2 bay leaves
- 1/2 teaspoon salt

Directions:

1) Place the beans in a bowl and cover with 3 inches of water. Soak the beans 4–8 hours. Once done drain.
2) Press the Sauté button of the Instant Pot® and add the oilto heat for 1 minute. Add the onion, jalapeño, and garlic and sauté until softened, about 5 minutes.
3) Add soaked beans, stock, tomato sauce, chili powder, mustard, oregano, cumin, pepper, bay leaves, and salt to the inner pot. Stir well to combine and scrape any brown bits from the bottom of the pot. Secure the lid.
4) Press the Manual or Pressure Cook button and adjust the time to 25 minutes.
5) Release pressure naturally until float valve drops and then unlock lid.
6) Remove and discard the bay leaves and then transfer the beans to a bowl for serving.

Chapter 3: 10 Savory Bean Soup

1. Italian Lentil Soup

Serves: 6

Cook Time: 55-60 minutes

Ingredients:

- 1 medium onion, chopped
- 1 tablespoon olive oil
- 2 garlic cloves, minced
- 3-1/4 cups water
- 1 can vegetable broth
- 1 cup dried lentils, rinsed

- 1 medium carrot, shredded
- 1 small green pepper, finely chopped
- 1 teaspoon dried oregano
- 1/2 teaspoon dried basil
- 1 can unsalted diced tomatoes
- 1 can tomato paste
- 1 tablespoon lemon juice
- 2 cups cooked brown rice
- 1/4 teaspoon crushed red pepper flakes, optional

Directions:

1) Turn on your Instant Pot and press the Sauté button. Put the onion and sauté for a while. Add in the garlic and stir for another minute.
2) Pour water, broth, lentils, carrots, and green pepper. Season the mixture with oregano, basil, and pepper flakes.
3) Use Manual/Pressure Cook button and set it to 20 minutes.
4) When the cooking cycle is complete, use the Quick-Release option to release the steam from the cooker.
5) Put the tomatoes, tomato paste, and lemon juice. Close the lid and turn the valve to Sealing. Click the Manual/Pressure Cook button and set it to 10 minutes.

6) When the cooking cycle is complete, use the Natural Release option to release the steam from the cooker.
7) Slowly open the lid. Check if the lentils are tender. Stir well.
8) Serve in bowls.

2. Instant Pot Soup Beans

Serves: 4-6

Cook Time: 60 minutes

Ingredients

- 2 cups dried pinto beans
- 4 cups low sodium vegetable broth
- 1/2 cup water
- 1 onion, diced
- 3 cloves garlic, minced

- 1 teaspoon onion powder
- 1 teaspoon ground cumin
- 1/2 teaspoon smoked paprika
- 1/4 teaspoon black pepper
- 3/4 teaspoon kosher salt

Directions:

1) Soak the beans in a basin of water for at least 2 hours before cooking.
2) Drain the beans and put them in the Instant Pot. Pour water to the pot.
3) Toss in onions, garlic, and broth and season with onion powder, cumin, and paprika while stirring.
4) Seal the pot and Click the Manual/Pressure Cook button and set it to 30 minutes.
5) When the cooking cycle is complete, use the Natural Release option to release the steam from the cooker.
6) Slowly open the lid and season ingredients with salt and pepper.
7) Serve in bowls with cornbread on the side
8) Season with salt and garnish as desired

3. White Bean and Ham Soup

Serves: 6

Cook Time: 30 minutes

Ingredients:

- 2 cans white beans, rinsed and drained
- 2 medium carrots, diced
- 1 small onion, chopped
- 2 tablespoons butter
- 2-1/4 cups water
- 1-1/2 cups fully cooked ham, cubed
- 1/2 teaspoon salt
- 1/8 to 1/4 teaspoon white pepper
- 1 bay leaf

Directions:

1) Pour one can of beans in a bowl. Mash and set aside.
2) Turn on your Instant Pot and press the Sauté button. Heat some butter, put the carrots and onions and sauté for several minutes.
3) Add the ham, bay leaf, mashed and whole beans. Pour water and season with salt and pepper.
4) Seal the lid and click the Manual/Pressure Cook button and set it to 10 minutes.
5) Use the Quick-Release option to release the steam from the cooker.
6) Remove the bay leaf.
7) Serve in bowls.

4. Instant Pot 15 Bean Soup

Serves: 8

Cook Time: 1 hour and 40 minutes

Ingredients:

- 1 package (20 oz.) Hurst's HamBeens 15 Bean Soup with seasoning packet
- 2 tablespoons vegetable oil
- 1 cup onion, chopped
- 1/2 cup celery, diced
- 2 cloves garlic, minced
- 2 quarts water
- 1 can (15 oz.) crushed tomatoes in puree
- 1/2 cup carrots, diced
- 1 teaspoon chili powder
- 2 cups spinach, roughly chopped
- 1 tablespoon lemon juice
- 1 cup diced ham, optional
- 1 ham bone, optional
- Salt and freshly ground black pepper to taste

Directions:

1) Wash and drain the beans.
2) Turn on your Instant Pot and press the Sauté button. Drizzle some oil and sauté the onion and celery. Stir for 3 minutes until the celery is tender.
3) Put the garlic and stir for another minute.

4) Add the beans and ham bone. Pour two quarts of water.

5) Seal the pot and click the Manual/Pressure Cook button and set it to 35 minutes on High Pressure.

6) Release pressure by using the Natural Release option to release the steam from the cooker.

7) Put tomatoes, carrots, chili powder, and seasoning packet.

8) Close the lid and turn on the pressure cook option. Cook on high pressure for 3 minutes.

9) Use the Natural Release option to release the steam from the cooker followed by Quick-Release option to release the remaining pressure.

10) Remove the ham bone. Add some spinach, cooked ham, and lemon juice and season as desired.

11) Serve in bowls.

5. Instant Pot Spicy Chicken Black Bean Soup

Serves: 8

Cook Time: 35 minutes

Ingredients:

- 2 tablespoon oil
- 1 large onion, finely chopped
- 2 celery stalks, finely chopped
- 1 red bell pepper, seeded and chopped
- 1 yellow bell pepper, seeded and chopped
- 400 g black beans, drained
- 800 g chopped tomatoes
- 2-3 cups corn
- 4 chicken breasts
- 2 tablespoon Cajun seasoning
- 2 teaspoons oregano

- 1 teaspoon paprika
- 1 teaspoon chilly flakes
- 2 teaspoon salt
- 1 teaspoon black pepper
- 3 cups chicken stock
- 2 teaspoon sugar (optional)

Directions:

1) Turn on your Instant Pot and press the Sauté button. Drizzle some oil and put the onion, celery, and bell peppers to the pot. Sauté them for several minutes.
2) When the vegetables are already soft, add the beans, corn, tomatoes, and chicken breasts. Season the mixture with Cajun, paprika, oregano, salt, and pepper.
3) Pour chicken stock, seal the lid and click the Soup button and set it to 10 minutes.
4) When the cooking cycle is complete, use the Quick-Release option to release the steam from the cooker.
5) Transfer the chicken breasts to a plate and shred. Afterwards, put the shredded chicken back to the soup.
6) Season to taste.
7) Serve in bowls. Top it with sour cream, chopped cilantro, and jalapeños.

6. Instant Pot Gumbo

Serves: 8

Cook Time: 45 minutes

Ingredients:

- 2 tablespoons olive oil
- 1 red bell pepper, diced
- 1 green bell pepper, diced
- 1 onion diced
- 1 cup celery, chopped
- 3 cloves garlic, minced

- 13.5 ounces Andouille sausage, cut into rounds
- 1/3 cup flour
- 1/3 cup butter
- 3 cups chicken broth
- 1 pound chicken, cubed
- 2 teaspoons Creole seasoning
- 10 ounces diced tomatoes with green chilies
- 14 ounces fire roasted diced tomatoes
- 2 bay leaves
- 1/2 teaspoon kosher salt
- 1/4 teaspoon black pepper
- 1 cup okra, sliced
- 1 pound shrimp peeled, deveined
- 4 cups cooked rice

Directions:

1) Turn on your Instant Pot and press the Sauté button. Drizzle some oil,sauté onion, garlic, bell peppers, celery, and sausage and cook for 3-5 minutes.
2) Once vegetables are soft and the sausage is cooked, remove them and set aside.
3) Dissolve butter on the pot. Add flour and stir constantly until it forms a roux. Turn off the pot.

4) Pour chicken broth. Put the cooked vegetables and sausage back to the pot, together with the chicken.
5) Add Creole seasoning, tomatoes with chilies, bay leaves ad season with salt and pepper.
6) Close the lid and move the valve to Sealing. Press the Manual/Pressure Cook button and set it to High Pressure. Cook it for 20 minutes.
7) When the cooking cycle is complete, use the Quick-Release option to release the steam from the cooker.
8) Add the okra and sauté okra cook for 5 minutes.
9) After 5 minutes, add the shrimp and cook for another 5 minutes.
10)   Pick out the bay leaves.
11)   Serve in bowls with rice on the side.

7. Black Bean Soup

Serves: 8–10

Cook Time: 60 minutes

Ingredients:

- 8 oz. slab or thick-cut bacon cut in small pieces
- 1 large red onion, chopped
- 2 medium carrots, coarsely chopped
- 6 garlic cloves, smashed
- 2½ teaspoon kosher salt
- 3 canned chipotle chilies in adobo
- 1 tablespoon adobo sauce
- 2 teaspoon dried oregano
- 1 teaspoon ground cumin
- 1 pound dried black beans, rinsed
- 2 tablespoon fresh lime juice

- For toppings: sour cream, corn chips, cilantro leaves, and lime wedges

Directions:

1) Turn on your Instant Pot and press the Sauté button sauté bacon for a while. When the bacon is already crispy, remove it using a slotted spoon.
2) Put half of the chopped onion in the pot, add carrots and garlic and season with salt. Stir well. Cook on Sauté function for several minutes until the vegetables are soft.
3) Stir in the chilies, adobo sauce, oregano, and cumin. Pour the beans and water and season with salt.
4) Seal the lid and press the Manual/Pressure Cook button and set it to High Pressure to cook it for 20 minutes.
5) When the cooking cycle is complete, use the Natural Release option to release the steam from the cooker.
6) Blend the mixture in   until the desired consistency is achieved.
7) In the meantime, combine lime juice and salt in a bowl. Stir well and add this to the soup. Stir again so that the flavor is distributed evenly.
8) Serve in bowls. Put sour cream, corn ships, cilantro, and pickled onion as toppings.

8. Instant Pot Red Beans and Rice Soup

Serves: 8

Cook Time: 1 hour and 30 minutes

Ingredients:

- 1 pound dried red beans
- 1 large onion, quartered
- 4 cloves garlic, peeled
- 1 green bell pepper, quartered
- 3 ribs celery, cut in thirds
- 7 cups water
- 3/4 cup uncooked brown rice
- 1 teaspoon salt
- 10 ounces tomatoes with chilies
- 1/4 teaspoon smoked salt
- Salt to taste
- seasoning mix

- 1 tablespoon smoked paprika
- 1 tablespoon dried thyme leaves
- 2 teaspoons dried oregano
- 1/2 teaspoon cayenne
- 1/2 teaspoon ground black pepper

Preparation:

Soak the beans in a basin of water overnight. Pre-soaked beans cook faster. If you were not able to soak them overnight, do a quick soak using your Instant Pot. Put the beans in the Instant Pot with 4 cups of water. Press the Sauté button and bring to a boil. Choose Manual/Pressure Cook option and set the timer to 2 minutes. Once the time is up, release the steam. Do not let the foam escape. If it escapes, seal the lid again for 20 seconds. Open the lid. Rinse and drain the beans. Set aside.

Directions:

1) Chop onions and garlic and them in a food processor. . Transfer them to a plate and set aside. Repeat the same procedure with the bell pepper and celery.
2) Turn on your Instant Pot and press the Sauté button and set it to medium heat. Sauté the finely chopped onion and garlic. Stir for several minutes. Then add the chopped pepper and celery. Stir continuously until the

vegetables are soft. Remove the mixture from the pot and set aside.

3) Pour the red beans, water, and rice to the pot. Season with salt. Add in half of the seasoning mix.

4) Close the lid and move the valve to Sealing. Press the Manual/Pressure Cook button and set it to High Pressure and cook it for 25 minutes.

5) Use the Natural Release option to release the steam from the cooker followed by Quick-Release function to release the remaining pressure.

6) Check if the beans are cooked. If the beans are still uncooked, cook them for another 5 minutes on high pressure. Then use the Quick-Release function to release the pressure from the cooker.

7) Stir in the vegetables and the remaining seasoning mix. Add the tomatoes. Pour small amount of water at a time until the desired consistency of the soup is achieved.

8) Press the Sauté button. Cook the soup for another 20 minutes, consistently stirring it and scraping the bottom of the pot.

9) Season with smoked salt to taste.

10)   Serve in bowls. Sprinkle chopped green onions on top.

9. Instant Pot Minestrone Soup

Serves: 8

Cook Time: 23 minutes

Ingredients:

- 1 small onion , about 1/3 cup, diced
- 2 cloves garlic , minced
- 1 medium carrot, chopped
- 1 large celery stalk, chopped
- 2 teaspoons dried basil
- 1 teaspoon dried oregano
- 3/4 teaspoon dried thyme
- 1 32-oz can diced tomatoes
- 3 tablespoons tomato paste
- 1 bay leaf

- 32 ounce carton, 4 cups low sodium vegetable broth
- water - add only as much as needed to cover vegetables
- 1/2 cup dry uncooked small shell pasta
- 1 medium zucchini, sliced into halves or quarters
- 1/2 cup canned or cooked red kidney beans
- 1/2 cup canned or cooked cannellini beans
- 1-2 cups fresh baby spinach/kale, chopped (optional)
- 1/2-1 teaspoon balsamic vinegar (optional)
- Shredded or grated Parmesan cheese (as topping)
- Fresh parsley, finely chopped (optional)

Directions:

1) 1Turn on your Instant Pot and press the Sauté button. Drizzle some oil and sauté onions and garlic for 3 minutes.
2) Put the carrots, celery, tomatoes, tomato paste, bay leaf, and dry pasta. Pour water and vegetable broth and season with basil, oregano, and thyme.
3) Close the lid and turn the valve to Sealing. Click the Manual/Pressure Cook button and set it to High Pressure for 2 minutes.

4) When the cooking cycle is complete, use the Quick-Release option to release the pressure from the cooker.

5) Toss in the zucchini, kidney beans, and cannellini beans.

6) Press the Sauté button. Cook the mixture for another 6 minutes until the pasta and beans are done.

7) Add the spinach/kale. Stir for a minute until they wilt. You may add small amounts of water at a time until the desired consistency is achieved.

8) Season to taste. Add some balsamic vinegar if it is available. This will definitely add flavor to your soup.

9) Serve in bowls and top with grated Parmesan cheese and chopped parsley.

10)   You can freeze the dish for future use. To avoid the pasta from getting soggy, separate it and the soup and store in separate container. Combine them and reheat when you are ready to serve.

10. Instant Pot Four Bean Beef Stew

Serves: 12

Cook Time: 1 hour and 15 minutes

Ingredients:

- 1/2 cup dried small red beans
- 1/2 cup black-eyed peas
- 1/2 cup navy beans
- 1/2 cup black beans
- 5 cups water
- 1/2 cup roasted peppers, chopped
- 2 tablespoon avocado oil
- 1 1/2 lb. stew meat
- 14 oz. can tomato sauce
- 1 14 oz. can diced tomatoes

- 1/2 tablespoon Montreal Seasoning
- 1/2 tablespoon marjoram
- 1/2 small cabbage, chopped
- 2 cups baby carrots

Directions:

1) Turn on your Instant Pot and press the Sauté button. Drizzle some oil and put the beans and pour water to the pot.
2) Click the Manual/Pressure Cook button. Set it on High Pressure. For newer version of Instant Pot, press the Bean function and set it to 25 minutes.
3) When the cooking cycle is complete, use the Quick-Release option to release the steam from the cooker.
4) Transfer the cooked beans to a bowl. Then wash the pot and dry.
5) Once the pot is dry, turn it on again. Turn on your Instant Pot and press the Sauté button ,drizzle the remaining avocado oil and braise the meat. Add the Montreal seasonings.
6) Toss the meat often. Cook it for 15 minutes until it turns brown.
7) With the exception of the beans, put all the remaining ingredients to the pot and stir well.
8) Click the Manual/Pressure Cook button. Put it on High Pressure. For newer version of the

Instant Pot, press the Meat function. Set it to 20 minutes.

9) After the cooking cycle is complete, Use the Natural Release option to release the steam from the cooker.

10)   Slowly open the lid. Add the beans to the meat. Stir well.

11)   Serve in bowls.

Chapter 4: 5 Sweet beans recipes and other desserts

1. Guilt-Free Chocolate Cake

Servings: 6

Cook Time: 70 minutes

Ingredients:

For the cake

- 8 ounces black beans
- 3 large eggs
- 1/2 tablespoon pure vanilla extract
- 1/4 teaspoon fine sea salt
- 3 tablespoons extra virgin coconut oil
- 1/4 cup raw honey
- 3 tablespoons cacao powder

- 1/2 teaspoon baking powder
- 1/4 teaspoon baking soda

For the glaze

- 1/4 cup dairy-free chocolate chips
- 1 tablespoon extra-virgin coconut oil

Directions:

1. 1Soak the beans in a basin of water overnight or at least four hours before you cook. Pre-soaked beans cook faster.
2. 2Rinse and drain the beans. Cook the beans. Put the black beans in the pot and pour water just enough to soak and cover the beans.
3. Close the lid and move the valve to Sealing. Press the Manual/Pressure Cook button and set it to High Pressure. Cook it for 12 minutes.
4. When the cooking cycle is complete, use the Natural Release option to release the steam from the cooker and let the beans cool.
5. Put all the cake ingredients, including the cooked beans, in a food processor. Pulse until the desired consistency is achieved.
6. Grease the cake pan and pour the batter and spread it on the pan.
7. Pour a cup of water to the pot and place the cake pan inside the pot.

8. Seal the pot and click the Manual/Pressure Cook button and set it to 45 minutes.
9. When the cooking cycle is complete, use the Quick-Release option to release the steam from the cooker. Allow the cake to cool.
10. In the meantime, combine coconut oil and dairy free chocolate chips in a bowl. Heat the mixture in a microwave for 45 seconds before you stir.
11. When the cake has cooled, carefully put it on a plate. Drizzle the glaze on top of the cake.
12. Serve and enjoy!

2. Red Bean and Coconut Milk Soup

Serves: 6-8

Cook Time: 50-60 minutes

Ingredients:

- 1 cup red beans
- ½ cup black glutinous rice
- 1 piece dried mandarin peel, store-bought or homemade
- 2 liter water
- Rock sugar, or to taste
- 90 gm. brown slab sugar, to taste

Directions:

1. Before starting to cook, remove the inner white of the mandarin peel, it tastes bitter.
2. Wash the beans and the glutinous rice and drain. Be sure to remove all excess liquid.
3. Combine all the ingredients in the pot And seal the valve. Press the Manual/Pressure Cook button and set it to High Pressure. For newer version of the Instant Pot, press the Porridge button.
4. When the cooking cycle is complete, use the Natural Release option to release the steam from the cooker.
5. Check if the red beans are soft and cooked. If you want your soup to be creamy and smooth,

cook it for another 15-20 minutes. Press the Sauté button and leave it uncovered.

6. Season the soup with salt and pepper. Stir well.

7. Serve in bowls.

3. Sweet Red Bean Paste

Serves: 6-8

Cook Time: 1 hour and 15 minutes

Ingredients:

- 1 pound dried red beans (adzuki beans)
- 3½ cups water
- 5 grams dried orange peel (optional)
- 1 cup vegetable oil
- Rock sugar (to taste)

Directions:

1. If you are using dried mandarin peel, place it in cold water before cooking. Leave it there for 15-20 minutes. Then remove the inner white of the peel . Meanwhile, wash the adzuki beans in running water and drain all liquid.
2. Put the adzuki beans (and the dried mandarin peel, if you are using it) in the Instant Pot and Pour 3 1/2 cups of water to cover the beans.
3. Seal the pot and click the Manual/Pressure Cook button and set it to 25 minutes. For newer versions of the pot, press Bean/Chili button. Cook for 25 minutes.
4. When the cooking cycle is complete, use the Natural Release option to release the steam from the cooker.
5. Transfer the beans together with the liquid to a food processor and Puree. For smaller food processors, do it by batch.
6. Place a medium saucepan on moderate heat , drizzle some oil,then put the puree and season it with sugar. Cook the mixture for 30-40 minutes. Stir occasionally to the bottom so the paste does not stick and burn on the pan. After at least 30 minutes, the mixture should become a very thick paste.

7. Season with sugar while stirring. Every 10 minutes, drizzle some oil. Make sure that the mixture absorbs the oil before you add more.
8. When the red bean paste can already hold its shape, it is cooked. Let it cool.
9. Serve and enjoy!

Storage: The sweet red bean paste can also be a filling. For future use, place it in an air-tight container. You can still use the red bean paste for a week.

4. Red Bean Soup with Mochi

Serves: 4

Cook Time: 1 hour and 35 minutes

Ingredients:

For the soup

- 1 1/4 cups red beans
- 8 cups water 1900ml
- 1/4 cup rock/ granulated sugar

For the mochi (10 pieces)

- 50 g shiratamako (or mochiko, 60g)
- 50 ml milk or soy milk
- 2 teaspoon sugar

Directions:

Cooking the soup:

1) Wash the red beans and drain water and put them in the Instant Pot.
2) Click the Manual/Pressure Cook button. Put it on High Pressure for 30 minutes.
3) When the cooking cycle is complete, use the Natural Release option to release the steam from the cooker. It should take several minutes for the pot to fully release the pressure.
4) Season ingredients with sugar and stir well.
5) Press Sauté button. Cook it for another 30 minutes. For a more creamy soup, press Normal. Cook for 30 minutes. For a watery soup, adjust the heat by pressing Adjust.

Choose Less. The beans should be cooked in a moderate simmer.

Making the mochi

1) Combine the sugar and glutinous rice flour in a bowl.
2) Pour some milk or water and mix gently . Knead it using your hands and form dough that is soft by adding water to achieve consistency.
3) Shape the dough into a small ball. Then indent the center using your index finger. Lay them neatly on a baking sheet so they will not touch each other.
4) Put them in boiling water. When the dough floats up, it is already cooked.
5) Immediately transfer them to a bowl with ice-cold water. Repeat the procedure to the rest of the dough.
6) Put the mochi to the pot of red beans soup.

Storage: You may freeze the mochi for future use. Transfer them to a Zip lock and store in a refrigerator. Boil them again when you are ready to use them.

5. Red Bean Soup

Serves: 6-8

Cook Time: 1 hour and 30 minutes

Ingredients:

- 1 cup adzuki beans/red mung beans
- 1 piece chenpi/dried mandarin peel
- 6 cups cold water
- 130g brown sugar
- 2 pinches kosher salt

Directions:

1) Place the dried mandarin peel in cold water. Leave it there for 15-20 minutes. Then remove the bitter   inner white of the peel. Meanwhile, wash the adzuki beans in running

water. Drain. Be sure to remove the excess liquid.

2) Put the beans and the mandarin peel in the Instant Pot. Pour 6 cups of water to cover the beans and season with salt and sugar.

3) Click the Manual/Pressure Cook button and set it to 30 minutes.

4) When the cooking cycle is complete, use the Natural Release option to release the steam from the cooker.

5) Slowly open the lid. Press the Sauté button. Simmer the beans for another 15-20 minutes, stirring occasionally and leave the pot uncovered.

6) Season while stirring continuously until you achieve the desired consistency of the soup.

7) Transfer it to a bowl and serve it as dessert. You may serve this sweet red beans soup warm or cold. Just pour coconut milk on top and it is good to go!

8) The sweet red beans soup can be chilled in refrigerator for future use. Leave it overnight in there overnight if you want to serve it cold the next day.

Conclusion

Nowadays, when human's life has become redundant physically and mentally, the quality of life is a top priority issue. One of the criteria to evaluate quality of life is the things that make the food that we eat in the body.

Many people tend to include more and more material derived from plants, especially cereals, such as corn kernels, almonds, macca seeds, cashews, ... because they know that science has proven amazing effects of these nuts on health. They can help the body create substances that prevent many diseases such as cancer, osteoporosis, high blood pressure, high cholesterol, ...

Beans are foods that contain more of these factors.

--Laura Summer

CPSIA information can be obtained
at www.ICGtesting.com
Printed in the USA
LVHW022141290323
743016LV00028B/942